Deptford Creek

First published in 1993 by
Cornerhouse Publications
70 Oxford Street
Manchester M1 5NH England
061 228 7621

in association with the
Museum of London
150 London Wall
London EC2Y 5HN
071 600 3699

ISBN 0 948797 77 0

Design and Artwork Production: Cornerhouse
Prints: Metro Photographic
Reprographics: Leeds Photo Litho
Print: Jackson Wilson

Printed on Sky Special Matt 170 gsm & 300 gsm

The staff at Cornerhouse for Deptford Creek are:
Dewi Lewis, Director
Niall Allsop, Design & Producton
Stephanie Taylor, Production Assistant
Alison Buchan, Sales & Distribution

A complete catalogue of Cornerhouse Publications is available on request

This book is published to coincide with the exhibition of the same name
at the Museum of London

Deptford Creek

Photographs by Jim Rice

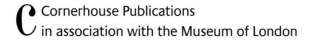
Cornerhouse Publications
in association with the Museum of London

museum of
LONDON

For Sadie, John, Sarah and Richard

Very special thanks to

Ron Richards, Jean and Dennis Hingston, Adrian Skirrow, Micky Lee, Benn Bond, Alex Pope, Dave Wall, John Payton, Debbie Sears, Dewi Lewis and Russell Clark without whose help and encouragement this project would never have got off the ground, let alone got this far.

Acknowledgements

AGFA, Ilford, Greenwich Reach Developments, Time Out Magazine, Metro Photographic, British Journal of Photography, the Independent, Coopers Metal, Pope & Bond, Brown & Mason Demolition, Hobson & Sons Ltd, the Hales Gallery Deptford, Photofusion Brixton, Cornerhouse, the Museum of London, Angela Simmonds, Stevie Robinson, Ruby Millington, Rev Canon Graham Corneck, Peter Gurnett, Mike Seabourne, Jo Clark, Christina Galustian and Adrian Tilley.

This project has been a joint effort between me and the people who live and work around the Creek. Even when they were working under very difficult conditions, I was never refused a photo opportunity – some people would take a very keen interest, 'Don't we need a flash on this one, Jim?' Or, when photographing one of their workmates who had just spent the day repairing the car fragmentiser: 'Chris, don't forget your make-up, love.' 'How does his eye shadow and lipstick look, Jim, are they the right shade?' And other such comments on their masculinity. This continued throughout, though the contact sheets give no clue to this behind-the-scenes banter. Everyone photographed took the situation in their stride, as if it were an everyday event.

On the technical side, I kept everything as simple as possible. Most of the portraits were shot on my old Rolleiflex, the rest on 35mm. Film was Ilford HP5+, printed on AGFA Record Rapid and developed in Neutol WA Print Developer. Debbie Sears of Metro Photographic produced the prints for both the exhibition and the book.

I must apologise to the people who have not been shown in the book or exhibition; there were just too many prints and Dewi Lewis had the difficult task of editing. All credit to the subject matter.

Deptford Creek

On the south side of the Thames, directly west of the many attractions of Greenwich, lies Deptford Creek. This little-known tributary of the Thames, seemingly cocooned from the world around it, still carries on its age-old calling as 'a working river'.

Deptford Creek, in fact, forms the three-quarter-mile stretch of the River Ravensbourne lying below Deptford Bridge. A bridge existed here by 1345, replacing the early 'Depe ford' which gave its name to the area west of the Creek.

Little evidence remains of the medieval settlement of fishermen, shipwrights, millers and farmers which clustered around St Nicholas's Church, Deptford Green, close to the river. With its medieval tower and seventeenth-century gateposts surmounted by stone skulls, St Nicholas's survived both the late Victorian clearances of much of old Deptford and bomb damage during the Second World War. The many sailors, shipwrights and local people buried in its churchyard bear silent witness to the area's rich historic past. Surprisingly, it is also here that the flamboyant Elizabethan dramatist, Christopher Marlowe, was buried after having been stabbed to death – in intriguing circumstances – at a tavern in Deptford Strand in 1593.

Deptford Strand was also the original headquarters (1514–1787) of the Corporation of Trinity House, responsible for pilotage and navigation lights on the Thames and British coasts. A short distance up-river, Henry VIII established Deptford Royal Dockyard in 1513. Sir Martin Frobisher sailed from here in 1576 to seek a north-east passage to China. The following year Francis Drake left on his voyage around the world, for which he was knighted in 1581 at Deptford by Queen Elizabeth I. His ship, the *Golden Hinde*, was laid up in the dockyard as a memorial before rotting away. Deptford-built ships also played an important part in the defeat of the Spanish Armada in 1588. Closer to the Creek itself, the newly formed East India Company began fitting out its fleet of merchant ships in 1601, effectively establishing the first flowering of the British Empire. By 1614 the Company had a shipyard, ironworks and extensive 'storage' facilities around the area still known as the 'Stowage'. During the second half of the seventeenth century, Samuel Pepys regularly visited Deptford Dockyard in the course of his Admiralty work. His good friend, the diarist and philosopher John Evelyn, lived nearby at Sayes Court. Czar Peter the Great came to Deptford in 1698 to learn shipbuilding techniques and he rented Sayes Court, with its remarkable botanical garden, from Evelyn.

By the eighteenth century Deptford was a prosperous and bustling shipping parish. One of London's finest baroque churches, St Paul's (1713–30), and one of London's earliest terraces at Albury Street (c. 1707–17) are physical reminders of Deptford's past wealth and grandeur. Other important surviving Georgian buildings are the Rum Warehouses and offices (1781–9) of the old Admiralty Victualling Yard, which operated on the site of the present Pepys Estate between 1742 and 1961.

During the nineteenth century Deptford became even more industrialised. Wharves, timber yards, engineering works, factories, mills and distilleries lined the Creek, and new privately owned shipyards and boilerworks appeared on the Thames waterfront. The world-famous General Steam Navigation Company had their repair yard at the Stowage between 1824 and the early 1970s. In 1836 London's first railway, the London to Greenwich Railway, reached Deptford. Just north of the Stowage, Deptford Power Station (built on the site of the Trinity House headquarters) opened in 1889. Designed by Sebastian de Ferranti to supply electricity to London, it was the world's first high-tension central generating station (it was replaced in the late 1940s and the whole site has recently been cleared). All of these operations, together with the coming and going of colliers and other shipping, actively contributed to the area's well-earned nickname of 'Dirty Deptford'. A wide range of skilled and semi-skilled workers found employment on the waterfront and Deptford had a busy social and community life.

Deptford Dockyard was one of London's largest industrial sites. However, it was too far from the sea and unsuitable for iron shipbuilding, and eventually closed in 1869. Between 1871 and 1913 the dockyard site operated as the Foreign Cattle Market, and later became a War Department supply depot. The site now forms part of the highly modernised Convoys Wharf, specialising in the handling and storage of imported newsprint.

Today, however, Deptford Creek quickly dispels the romantic view of the working river. Amongst the inherited dereliction of the 1980s, demolition contractors and scrap dealers ply their trade, welders repair refuse barges, ships are loaded with anything recyclable and cranes unload aggregates for the building trade. A dying industrial landscape awaits the end of the recession and the hand of the developer.

Soon Deptford Creek is likely to merge anonymously with the other Docklands and riverside developments. Few of the two million people who visit Greenwich each year ever take the short walk to Deptford. Yet here is a stretch of waterfront rich in the vein of an extraordinary and real history – a history which is largely unrecognised and ignored.

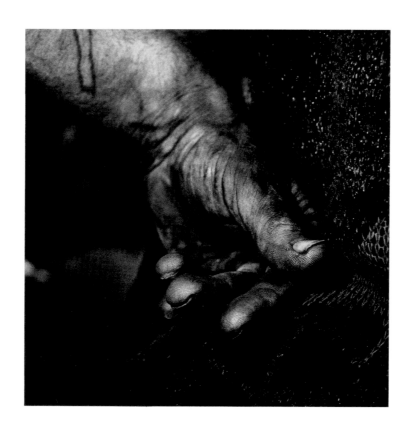

Locations

7   St Nicholas's Church
9   Scrap dealer's hand, Micky's Yard
11 View of boat leaving the Creek after unloading sand
12 View of the Creek
13 The London Marathon
15 Dave repairing part of the Creek
16 Welders repairing the Creek
17 Scrambles, Coopers Metal
18 Young Billy, Stowage Metal
19 Paul, Stowage Metal
20 Paul repairing lorry clutch
21 Customer looking for spares, Micky's Yard
22 John, welder, Pope & Bond
23 Eddy, ARC Aggregates
24 Brian, welder, Pope & Bond
25 Arthur, Coopers Metal
26 Customer looking for spares, Micky's Yard
27 Customer, Stowage Metal
28 Tony, Coopers Metal
29 Ron, welder, Pope & Bond
30 Richard repairing car frag machine
31 Seamus repairing frag machine
32 Bill demolishing Deptford Power Station
33 Saturday boy
34 Mike Canty's son and friend playing by the Thames
35 Car boot sale, burger bar
36 Axles, Micky's Yard
37 Car spares
38 Thirty-year-old rivets, Pope & Bond
39 ARC tar storage tank
41 ARC in snowstorm view from Coopers

42 Power station with original Ferranti arches still intact; Micky's Yard in foreground
43 The Creek
44 The Stowage
45 Neil rescues his grab from fire
46 Richard, major overhaul of car frag machine, Coopers
47 Stowage Metal, melting down aluminium engines
48 Repairing car frag machine, Coopers
49 Chris cutting up lorry, Micky's Yard
50 ARC demolition men moving steel rope
51 Eddie stabling horse
52 Fire at Coopers, Green Watch, Deptford Fire Station
53 Fire at Coopers, Green Watch, Deptford Fire Station
55 Pope & Bond, repairing the tug (*Jean Raby*)
56 Pope & Bond, repairing inside of barge
57 Coopers, repair crew next to car frag machine
58 Power station, first drop, police officers, traffic control
59 Power station, first drop, group shot
61 Power station, start of the demolition
62 Power station, inside view
63 Top-cutters, power station
64 Main floor section, power station
65 Pete, top-cutter
66 First drop. The object at the top of the picture landed in Deptford High Street
67 The end of an era ... a different explosive company finally drops Deptford's most famous landmark
69 The skip ... the history of Deptford Power Station?
70 Old bricks from the power station, crushed and ready to fill in the crater
71 ARC demolition